Little Lady

Written by Elissa Stacy
Illustrated by Donna Stackhouse

Hey There little lady
I have something for you.

It's a very special secret
meant just for you.

You see this beautiful lady
standing beneath the tree.

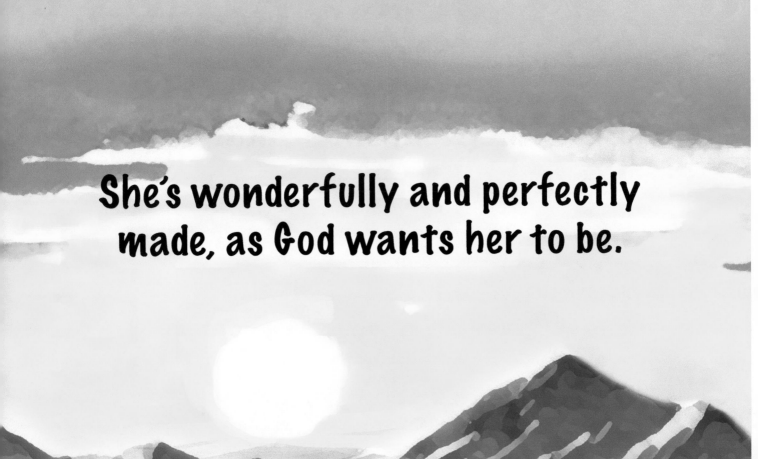

She's wonderfully and perfectly made, as God wants her to be.

She's talented, she's smart and lots of fun, too.

She's big, she's bold, she's bright, and filled with lots of might.

She's loving and kind,
successful and honest.

She'll always do her best cuz
that's her promise

She's joyful and peaceful,
and encouraging too.

She's friendly to everyone she meets and is always there for you.

She leads with her heart
because she knows that's true.

Why am I telling you this, you ask
Why is she important to you?

Because Little Lady,
That Woman...

Little Lady

Publishing services by:
Telemachus Press, LLC
7652 Sawmill Road, Suite 304
Dublin, Ohio 43016

Author's website:
www.StacyCoDesigns.com

Follow the author on Facebook:
www.facebook.com/elissa.stacy.3

ISBN: 978-1-956867-20-6 (eBook)
ISBN: 978-1-956867-21-3 (paperback)

Library of Congress Control Number: 2022900477

Version: 2022.01.11

TELEMACHUS PRESS